TANTRIC SEX

Discover The Path of Sacred Sex And
The Ultimate Pleasure That Awaits You
and Spice Up Your Sex Life

Todd Martinez

TANTRIC SEX

Discover The Path of Sacred Sex And The Ultimate
Pleasure That Awaits You and Spice Up Your Sex Life

Todd Martinez

All rights are reserved.

CONTENTS

Chapter 1

THE ORIGIN OF TANTRA

According to some sources, Tantra has been practiced in India for more than 5,000 years. "Weave together" is the Sanskrit word for "woven together." Tantric sex is practiced by Buddhist and Hindu devotees as a way to "weave" the physical and spiritual, according to some sources.

When it comes to sexual intimacy, the importance of intimacy is underlined because it combines spirituality with the act of having a sexual relationship.

Tantra, on the other hand, is not just about having a good time. More than anything else, it is all about celebrating your body and enhancing your sense of sexiness. Meditation, sexuality, and spirituality are all intertwined in this form of spirituality. You can enjoy it alone or with a partner, depending on the situation. It promotes sensual experiences.

The ultimate goal of tantric sex is to have a sensual experience while also achieving spiritual or energetic contact.

It takes time, and the goal is not always to make the other person orgasm. You are instead looking for a deeper connection with your partner or with yourself on a more profound level. Breathing, sound, and movement are all necessary to activate sexual energy.

The ancient field of Tantra is so vast that it is impossible to cover it all here. Traditional Yoga practices are included, but so are practices that have been deemed a threat to society's established codes and standards at times. Tantra's sexual practices fall into this highly controversial category.

Human sexuality is an integral part of the overall process while engaging in practices that aim to speed up the natural transformation of human spirituality in humans.

Using our sexuality as a complement to a comprehensive system of yoga practices is the focus of this book. This book teaches couples and solo practitioners how to cultivate ecstatic energy to its highest levels of spiritual manifestation in support of the journey toward sexual emancipation.

It is the goal of this work to present the most effective methods of spiritual practice in a series of easy-to-read books that anyone can use to gain immediate and long-term practical results in their lives. It is broken down into three sections: Over the course of centuries, these potent practices have been taught in secrecy, with the primary goal of ensuring their continued existence in the modern world. Due to the fact that we are living in the information age, we have the ability to preserve knowledge for present and future generations in ways that were previously unthinkable. "Can we go as far as we possibly can in terms of effectively transmitting spiritual methods through writing?" is a question that continues to be asked.

Chapter 2

INTRODUCTION

Sexual experiences have a profound effect on a person's spiritual development. The term "tantra" has become synonymous with "spiritual sex" in recent years. However, tantra is far more than a sexual experience. In terms of spiritual practices, it is probably the most comprehensive in the world, covering everything from yoga to tai chi without omitting anything. Tantric practices have received a "bad rap" because they encompass not only meditation and breathing techniques but also sexual practices such as pranayama (yogic breathing). And, of course, "Tantra is about sex!" we proclaim as human beings. Tantric analysis typically proceeds along sexual lines, for better or worse.

This is why we will discuss tantra in terms of sexual aspects rather than other aspects, as sex plays a unique role in spiritual practices and our ascension to higher states of consciousness. You cannot be happy or fulfilled in life if you ignore this. As a result, we are including sex in this book. Then, we demonstrate the connection between tantric sexual principles and other traditional aspects of yoga.

Sex, according to conventional wisdom, is not a hindrance to spiritual development. Rather than being an adversary, sex can be a valuable ally if it is recognized for what it is and utilized effectively. This can be accomplished in a variety of ways, each tailored to the preferences of individual spiritual practitioners. The underlying principle in each case is the cultivation of pre-orgasmic sexual energy with the goal of long-term manifestation of our inherent ecstatic nature. Once we have even a sliver of what it is like, an entirely new realm of possibility begins to emerge within us. This is in contrast to reproductive sex's transient nature.

It is fascinating to observe how a perception changed as tantra gained acceptance in contemporary society. There is a widespread belief that tantra is about sex; indeed, the vast majority of people today believe that tantra is entirely about sex. As a result, the rallying cry of tantric practitioners has become "Sex, sex, sex!" Is it because we have a fixed mindset, or is there something else at work? This is entirely normal. The climactic sex act, particularly the intense pleasure of orgasm, is the climax of the majority of people's lives. As a result, it is unsurprising that we live in a sexually obsessed society, whether we like it or not. We are all aware that sex acts as a gateway to a more primal part of ourselves. Sex is the glue that holds us together in terms of love, family, and spirituality. As a result, we are naturally drawn to sex. It is the foundation of everything we are. We are who we are as a result. Our deepest desires are to become inextricably linked to the ecstasy of "sex" and never leave.

The ultimate mystery of sex can be solved only by adopting a broad perspective on the subject. This is where tantra comes into play.

What would you think if I told you that tantra is all about sitting and meditating? Tantra does, in fact, address these concerns primarily. Yes, sex is a component of tantra, and we must confront it head on if we wish to continue on our path. We miss out on the opportunity to connect with our inner divine self and the world around us when we exclude sexuality from our yoga practice. Sexual energy's contribution to the development of our nervous system in this direction cannot be overstated.

Tantra is a Sanskrit term that translates as "woven together" or "two fullnesses as one." This entails a yoga-like union with an emphasis on intimacy. Tantra requires the ecstatic fusion of two poles: father heaven and mother earth, masculine and feminine energies such as shiva and shakti, and yin and yang. Tantra recognizes that these two poles are contained within us, in our nervous system. On a daily basis, we see the results of this.

It is the most inclusive of all yoga systems because it views life as a synthesis of two realities contained within the human nervous system.

Tantra yoga comes in a variety of forms, including mantra, kriya, kundalini, and hatha yoga. Tantra's "right-handed side" refers to the practices associated with these traditional yoga systems. By contrast, the left-handed approach to tantra yoga seeks to infuse the material world with pure bliss consciousness through sensual life practice. Left-handed individuals do not shy away from savoring the finer things in life. Indeed, they are spiritually beneficial in this way. As with yoga's dark side, it is best to avoid the left-handed side at all costs. For the simple reason that this is the conventional wisdom. This was the case prior to the hipster generation gaining access to tantra. Nowadays, it is considered acceptable to practice tantra with the left hand. It is, at the very least, in the Western developed world. Perhaps Westerners have nothing to fear, given their pre-existing enslavement to materialism. It is past time for us to incorporate spirituality into our daily lives. Permit us to consume both the cake and the icing concurrently. A tantra for the left hand is clearly visible.

As a result, this book focuses on the sexual methods of left-handed tantra.

The article discusses Kundalini, the vast latent energy inherent in our sexual biology that can be systematically awakened and managed through advanced yoga practices. These practices are incorporated into our twice-daily sitting practices, which are centered on deep meditation and spinal breathing pranayama. These practices assist in continuously propelling ecstatic sexual energy upward and into our nervous system, and they are incorporated into our overall sitting practice routine. Additionally, asanas, mudras, and bandhas are spiritual transformation practices that are aimed at enhancing the role of our sexual energy in the process of spiritual transformation.

All of these sitting practices have a beneficial effect on the body from the ground up (perineum). We are going to get down to the nitty-gritty of tantric sexual methods. This is an absolute necessity. Because if we do not gain control over the massive flows of prana (life force) that occur during the sex act, we may discover that our ability to achieve spiritual goals in our nervous system is limited. Clearly, this does not require us to consider the dreaded "C" word – celibacy. Indeed, we will consider some intelligent methods for more closely aligning our sexual activities with our spiritual aspirations. Indeed, you may be surprised to learn that intelligent spiritual sex can be far more pleasurable than the conventional type of sex that begins with the phrase "Wham bam, thank you Ma'am."

Is there a way to determine our readiness for tantric sexual techniques? It is not at all difficult. We will desire sexual activity that is naturally regenerative in nature. It will be significant for us. The more we desire something, the more likely we are to obtain it. This desire is referred to as Bhakti. The presence of bhakti in our lives is readily apparent, as is the presence of bhakti in the lives of others.

This occurs as a result of the nervous system's purification as a result of our yoga practices. It is a kind of magnetism that develops within us, beckoning us toward something greater. A compelling call is required to compel us to engage in a new spiritually oriented mode of sexual activity, because we must embark on something truly revolutionary. To engage in tantric sex, a strong desire for it is required. We are about to embark on an adventure that will alter the course of a powerful river. We are taught in tantric sex to engage in sex for the purpose of cultivating sexual energy upward, rather than for the sake of orgasm, and to subordinate our deeply ingrained obsession with orgasm. Sexual energy is spiritually cultivated first, followed by orgasm – a significant shift in our expectations. We will be able to expand our sexual functioning into a cultivating mode in the presence of a strong desire, just as we train our arousal, which has been elevated through certain sitting practices, to a much higher level of functioning over time. Tantric sex is comparable in that it requires gradual training over time. Tantric sex is not a quick fix. It is the result of months and years of gradual development. This will occur as our bhakti strengthens, as it is required for us to complete our journey to enlightenment.

Each individual's sexual journey through yoga will be unique. Each of us will have an experience as unique as our sexual preferences.

There is no compelling reason for those with a light to moderate sex life to incorporate yogic methods into their sexual relationships; however, learning tantric sex will undoubtedly improve our lovemaking abilities, as well as our overall yoga practice. With the assistance of the occasional fling, it is not difficult to attain enlightenment. Yoga's traditional methods (for example, right-handed tantra) will more than suffice to accomplish the task at hand.

It is a different story for those who are extremely sexually active. However, despite the fact that the pelvis contains an enormous amount of prana (life force), there are limits to how much prana can be expelled while remaining spiritually vibrant. This is especially true for men, as orgasm results in the release of large amounts of prana along with the ejaculation of sperm, which is extremely beneficial. It is also true to a degree for women, though not to the same degree. Because he is the one who loses the most prana during orgasm, he is the key to tantric sex. As a result, he also determines the duration of the sexual union and, consequently, the amount of sexual energy that can be developed during the act of lovemaking (lovemaking duration). The extent to which a woman's bhakti (desire) to increase sexual energy in herself and her partner can be accomplished in a sexual union is determined by her bhakti; however, the extent to which a man's bhakti can be achieved is determined by his bhakti. As a result, the roles of man and woman in tantric sex are somewhat distinct. In another sense, their roles, however, are identical. Neither man nor woman can engage in tantric sex unless they both actively participate in the intelligent management of the man's ejaculatory flow. This is true during the initial stages of learning tantric sex and for a period of time afterwards.

Once a man has gained control of his sperm and is no longer dependent on his partner to control his ejaculation, he can become self-sufficient. Once both partners achieve this level of proficiency, they can virtually indefinitely cultivate sexual energy preorgasmically. Each of us has encountered Asian visual art depicting tantric lovers in union, whether performing musical instruments, reading poetry, or engaging in an extended loving conversation. This is not typically what we think of as sex in the Western world, or even tantric sex. However, this is what authentic tantric sex is all about: the prolonged cultivation of sexual energy in lovemaking prior to the orgasmic cycle.

It is necessary to emphasize a few points.

To begin, tantric sex is not an end in and of itself. It is insufficient as a stand-alone yoga practice. Tantric sex is an ineffective practice for cleansing and opening the nervous system on a global scale. This will not work. In this case, the most critical tools to employ are deep meditation and spinal breathing pranayama. After the body has been cleansed, yoga asanas, mudras, bandhas, and kumbhaka (breath suspension) are all extremely effective at directing sexual energy upward. As a result, the sushumna (the spinal nerve that runs from the bottom of the pelvis to the brain) and the hundreds of thousands of nerves that branch off from the spine and reach every part of the body during the experience experience an increase in ecstatic conductivity. Tantric sex, particularly in the case of sexually active yogis and yoginis, may contribute to this process (a yogi is a male practitioner of yoga, and a yogini is a female practitioner).

Having tantric sex does not imply that we are attempting to increase our sexual arousal. If we already engage in sexual activity, there is something we can do to strengthen our yoga practice. As a result, this discussion is not intended to encourage everyone to engage in more tantric sex. If you engage in light to moderate sex and are satisfied with your yoga practice, your physical and mental health are excellent. Avoid sexual encounters solely for the purpose of reading the content on this website. Those who are already sexually active and seeking ways to incorporate their sexual activity into the larger scope of their yoga practice will benefit from this book on tantric sex.

Second, some may believe it is a bad idea to put orgasm on hold while we work on developing the ability to cultivate sexual energy indefinitely upward. In this situation, it may appear as though we are throwing the baby out with the bathwater. After all, orgasm is the most intense form of pleasure we have ever known. This is a legitimate and understandable concern, and we are perfectly justified in asking, "How about orgasm?" "Could you tell me what becomes of it?"

This is not anti-orgasm writing. Indeed, it is a path of pleasure, an ecstatic path. Orgasm is a physiological ecstasy induced by a specific type of stimulation – sexual stimulation that is biologically oriented toward reproduction. The condition that we refer to as enlightenment is also an ecstatic response in the body elicited by a particular type of stimulation – stimulation elicited by yoga practices that are biologically oriented toward the birth of our awareness in unending pure bliss consciousness and divine ecstasy.

Is orgasm sacrificed for enlightenment? No, enlightenment is the flowering of orgasm, its expansion into an endless state of full bloom throughout the entire body.

According to Ramakrishna, a great 19th-century Indian sage, divine ecstasy is analogous to an infinite number of yonis (female sex organs) engaged in continuous orgasm in every atom and pore of our body.

Thus, while it may appear at first that we are relegating something vital to the back burner, what we are actually doing is gradually expanding our orgasmic response into cosmic realms via our purifying and opening nervous system. There, we discover that ecstasy has no bounds in terms of magnitude or duration. It is simply a matter of cultivating our nervous system in order to bring to light what is already within us.

All of this is accomplished through our bhakti/desire. Each day, we make a new choice about our path.

Now, let us delve into the specifics of tantric sex practices.

Chapter 3

MYTH

Tantra is a form of spirituality that transcends sexual orientation. It is a subfield of Eastern philosophy that deals with a wide range of esoteric ideas.

In order to increase one's sexual desire, one can use tantric techniques such as breathing, yoga, and meditation. One common myth about tantric sex is that it involves wild, unrestrained sexual encounters. This is not how it should be. Even though tantric techniques can open you up to new experiences, they are more of a mental than a spiritual endeavor.

Many people believe that practicing tantra is always best done with a partner. Individual tantric sex is possible, despite the fact that many couples participate in tantric sex.

A tantric experience does not necessitate genital contact or intercourse, in fact. It is true that engaging in sexual activity can heighten your sensual experience, but tantric practices can help you deepen your connection to your own body and mind while also providing pleasurable experiences for yourself.

Indeed, those who practice tantric techniques or follow the tantric path are aiming for the ultimate goal of soul liberation and consciousness expansion through their practice of the tantric techniques. Tantric sex is one option, but there are many others.

The practitioner does not have to bend into awkward positions as some people believe in order to engage in tantric sex. The term "intimacy" refers to a level of physical closeness between two people that is mutually agreeable. Every move, every touch, everything is completely at your discretion, both physically and verbally.

Chapter 4

DIFFERENCE WITH NEO TANTRA

When looking for information on tantric sex, the terms tantra, tantric sex, and neotantra are frequently used together (new tantra). Despite the fact that the terms tantra and neotantra are frequently used interchangeably, it is important to understand the subtle differences between the two.

tantra is an ancient Eastern practice that has been practiced for over 5,000 years and is still going strong today. The term "neotantra" refers to a modernized Westernized form of tantra, such as the Islamic State.

Neo Tantra is a modern interpretation of ancient tantric texts in the context of the New Age movement. As a result, neo Tantra incorporates some unconventional practices and techniques that are not always used by practitioners of traditional tantra.

Chapter 5

PRACTICES IN TANTRIC SEX

One of the most fundamental principles that underpins all tantric sexual practices, no matter how they are carried out, is the preorgasmic cultivation of sexual energy. It is possible to combine traditional sitting yoga with solo sexual practice when doing it with a partner. We will go into more depth on each of these topics in the sections that follow. In order to begin, however, something must be established a priori (before the fact). That something is a desire to be fulfilled. To make significant progress with tantric sexual methods, we need a strong desire for something more (also known as bhakti). This desire must be present before we can make significant progress.

There are a few ways to prepare for tantric sex prior to engaging in it. The first step is to create an environment conducive to growth and learning. When practicing tantric techniques, it is critical to be in an environment that is both comfortable and distraction-free. Once you have located the ideal location, it is time to unwind and settle in.

Individuals are urged to view mindful sex as a long, meandering walk rather than the breathless sprint to the finish that orgasm-focused intercourse can be. According to her, there is no prohibition against orgasm, and individuals may engage in them whenever they please. "However, that is not the objective you have set." It is preferable to spend (a great deal of) time getting to know one another than to rush into penetration before a woman's body is ready, and Richardson believes that scheduling sex can have a foreplay-like effect on men by creating anticipation.

The Power of Intention

Many people believe that we must have a constant desire for something and be willing to take daily action in order to achieve it. Our actions are fueled by a sense of direction and direction comes from a purpose. Take a moment to think about some of the most successful people you know. There is a striking resemblance between the two of them. There is no doubt that they have dedicated a significant amount of time and effort into becoming the best at what they do. For years, they persevered, overcoming obstacles, and working toward their goal because they had an insatiable desire to see it through. This is similar to tantra, which aims to awaken and unite the soul with the divine.

Jesus said, "Blessed are those who thirst and hunger for righteousness." "Seek and ye shall find" was another of his sayings. "Open the door automatically by knocking."

Having a burning desire to achieve a goal, and then taking action toward that goal, is the magic formula for success. Insatiable cravings are the driving force behind this behavior. The fuel for the fire is provided by daily action. It is crucial to use the words "goal" and "continuous." Desires become dispersed, actions become unfocused, and little happens as a result of the absence of these two key operative functions. The sky is the limit when you have them on your side.

An individual's desire to pursue a specific goal, such as attaining divine union through tantric means through constant focus, is a unique type of cultivation. It is called devotion, after all. An object or goal can be defined as a constant source of desire if one is dedicated. Devotion is something we have all heard of. The following is how we explain the success of high achievers: It is obvious that she is devoted to her work. According to great mystics, "Oh, she is dedicated to God," this young woman is. The fact that devotion and greatness are found in the same place, the heart, is no accident. When one comes after the other, it is a given. In order for the second to occur, the first must take place.

Enlightenment and sexual fulfillment can come in many forms, and it is up to you to find the one that resonates with you the most. It is the driving force behind all of our work. As a result, we are able to practice spirituality for a longer period of time each day. Our relationship with God deepens and deepens as we practice. Commitment to one's spiritual life is strengthened by increased devotion, which in turn strengthens one's commitment to practice. Practicing devotion leads to having a divine experience and increasing one's level of devotion; this is how it all goes down. As a spiritual seeker, devotion is your best friend and must be maintained at all times. Spiritual hunger and thirst are not always easy, but they are necessary if we are going to progress on the royal path toward enlightenment. Because of our unwavering dedication to transforming our lives through yoga and tantric methods, we can be sure that whatever needs to be done, will be done.

The Holdback Technique – A Stairway to Heaven

What does the term "perfection of lovemaking" mean? Is it possible to have a free lunch? It is analogous to the question, "What is enlightenment?" Alternatively, "What is wisdom?" It is possible that they are interchangeable. Finally, it makes no difference what they are; we must begin from where we are. There is a process we can follow, a journey we can embark on. It is possible to begin where we are and progress forward if we believe that something more exists. To successfully complete the journey, one must possess an intense desire to do so.

Sexual relationships are influenced by a plethora of factors. Compatibility cannot be overstated. Are we having a good time together? Are we at ease with each other in bed? Personal preference and style have numerous nuances, and we are constantly on the lookout for ways to tailor them to our liking. Is it accurate to say that I am attractive? Is he/she aesthetically pleasing? Is flirting acceptable? Is the foreplay satisfactory? Is the location in which you intend to have sexual relations appropriate – your bedroom, the basement, or the kitchen table?

These are topics that we will not spend a great deal of time discussing in this section. Without a doubt, they are significant. However, it is the act itself that we wish to focus on here. Specifically, we will discuss how sexual stimulation affects prana (our life force expressed as sexual energy) and how we can incorporate it into our yoga practice. It goes without saying that this process is not complete without addressing the question, "What do I want from sex?" Assuming the answer is "something other than genital orgasm," we can begin investigating tantric sexual methods.

The procedures are relatively simple. It is concerned with sexual stimulation and orgasm control. And it is related to male plumbing (piping). When you stop to consider it, it is quite banal. However, as you know, we bring a lot of baggage to the bed with us – for example, our sex obsessions. And this can add to the complexity. It is not necessary, however, to be complicated.

We have obsessive sex-related thoughts and strong emotional reactions that we are powerless to control. Keep in mind that we are in the bed for a higher purpose in lovemaking, and allow our sexual obsessions to be directed toward that higher purpose through bhakti/desire. A little devoutness can go a long way.

A critical component of this higher purpose is remembering that tantric sex is about our partner's needs, and this is a critical component of remembering. If both partners embrace this, they will have great success in tantric sex, or in any sex, or in any relationship. It is comparable to a Buddhist koan, which is an unsolvable riddle. Who is served if both partners seek to serve the other? What is the need that has been met if a person's personal need has been met?

Naturally, giving our all to our partner is the ideal, and it is a goal that will be gradually achieved over time. Allow your attention to naturally wander to it occasionally while you are sharing a bed. It will have a noticeable effect. If approached with sincerity, the goal of tantric sex is to honor and fill your partner with divine ecstasy (which you most likely already had in mind). As such, take this as confirmation of what you intuitively understand. Tantric sex is all about the relationship between you and your partner. Naturally, there will be times when neither partner shares the same level of concern for the other. That is acceptable to me. Giving does not require the exchange of goods or services in return. Lovemaking is not comparable to business transactions.

The act of creating "love" is the act of creating "love." Giving and receiving love are two distinct concepts. We make love by doing something for someone else without expecting anything in return. This is the essence of love. A long-term commitment is not always necessary. It is not concerned with the future or the past; it is concerned with the present. It is simply a matter of being present in the moment.

When it comes to making love, sometimes the best course of action is to say "no." Being in love does not require us to give in to every desire our partner has, especially if that desire is destructive. Saying "no" in these circumstances is also a sign of love and respect. It is not for the faint of heart to fall in love. Love is a prudent decision. Love is a mighty force. The peace and light that love brings benefit all of life. This is a critical aspect of the tantric sexual experience we wish to cultivate. It will occur naturally over time.

As a result, the following are the fundamental components:

To begin, it is critical to understand that tantric sex is about cultivating sexual energy directed upward pre-orgasmically in our nervous system. Second, that the sitting yoga practices discussed in other AYP writings (meditation, pranayama, and so on) can assist in purifying the nervous system in preparation for yoga practice. Thirdly, we are looking for more than genital orgies. Fourthly, we are always accessible to our partner.

For the time being, let us discuss the holdback method.

The male organ is called the lingam, and the female organ is called the yoni. These are the traditional Sanskrit names for the masculine and feminine organs of regeneration used in tantra. They encompass the entire spectrum of ecstatic union, from the physical to the most spiritual levels of consciousness.

When the man is on top and the woman is at the bottom of the stack, the holdback method is easiest to perform.

Scan, let go, and repeat.

Take your time, focusing on each area of your body—jaw, shoulders, belly, genitals, and buttocks—and using your breath to soften any tight areas you notice. Your stomach begins to relax as soon as you embrace your partner. After that, there is your jaw. After that, if you look again, you will notice, oh! That has been tightened up yet again! It is simply the way we are by nature. As a result, scanning and softening continue." This should be done both during and after your tantric session as a means of reconnecting with your own body and mind.

"When a man moves slowly, it enables a woman to trust the situation, relax, and open up," the author explains.

According to Richardson, "the pelvic floor is a classic area where we tighten." Women may notice that they tense up when they lose track of time and become lost in thought. According to the actress, she can "be engaged with a man inside and suddenly notice, oh, I am holding my vagina a little tight." "These patterns of contraction are simply there." It is simply a matter of remembering the facts." Take note of any tension and release it with a deep breath.

Meditation

All it takes is a brief pause to be aware of your surroundings, regardless of whether or not you have ever meditated before. Make full use of your five senses to take in everything around you.

Breathing

Exhale slowly and completely to remove all remaining air from your lungs. It is important to keep doing this until you get the hang of it. A tantric breathing goal is to inhale deeply enough to begin experiencing sensation in your genital area.

Movement

Release any tension in your body by lying flat on your back. As you inhale, arch your back and raise your pelvis. Continue doing this until you feel calmer and more in touch with your body and emotions, and then build on it until it becomes second nature.

Tantric sex is a popular pastime for many couples who want to deepen their relationship. With the help of tantric techniques, you and your partner can develop close, intimate contact while also exploring each other's bodies and enhancing your sexual attraction to each other. Discovering your true passions with your partner will benefit both of you, and you will be able to pass on your knowledge to your partner along the way.

As with all forms of sexual pleasure, tantric sex is meant for a long and satisfying experience. In order to get the most enjoyment out of their partner's closeness and intimacy, many people try to keep orgasm at bay for as long as possible.

If you and your partner are ready to explore tantric sex, practicing eye contact is essential. For the first few minutes, face your partner and maintain eye contact while still wearing your clothes. Improve your ability to breathe in time with your movements by practicing various breathing techniques. Tantric techniques can be incorporated into your practice after you have established a regular rhythm.

As soon as you have stripped down to your underwear, you can start touching, sensing, and moving with your partner in whatever manner feels most natural to you. The most important thing to remember is to maintain eye contact and keep your attention on your breathing. Nothing else matters except being fully present in the moment and savoring each and every sensation that comes your way.